THE ADVENTUROUS LIFE OF A VERSATILE ARTIST HOUDINI

THE ADVENTUROUS LIFE OF A VERSATILE ARTIST HOUDINI

HARRY HOUDINI

ISBN: 978-93-88321-05-1

First Published: -

LECTOR HOUSE LLP
E-MAIL: lectorpublishing@gmail.com

THE ADVENTUROUS LIFE
OF A VERSATILE ARTIST
HOUDINI

BY

HARRY HOUDINI

THE WORLD FAMOUS SELF-LIBERATOR

HOUDINI,

Presenting the Greatest Performance of his Strenuous Career, liberating himself after being Locked in a

WATER TORTURE CELL

(Houdini's own Invention) whilst Standing on his Head, his Ankles Clamped and Locked above in the centre of the Massive Cover.

A FEAT WHICH BORDERS ON THE SUPERNATURAL

$1,000

HOUDINI offers this sum to any one proving that it is possible to obtain air in the upside-down position in which he releases himself from this

WATER FILLED TORTURE CELL.

CONTENTS

Six Million of these Books in circulation since 1900, in various Forms, Editions and Languages.

HOUDINI

THE ADVENTUROUS LIFE OF A VERSATILE ART-IST.

(Revised 1922 Edition).

HARRY HOUDINI, "the World's Handcuff King and amazing Prison Breaker," a title universally and unanimously bestowed upon him, has had a career as adventurous and romantic as the most imaginative writer could possibly conjure.

Indeed, this wonderful genius, with a science concerning bolts, bars, locks, and chains that will yet revolutionize the world's methods of safeguarding itself against "the men that prowl in the night," confirms the truth of the ancient adage that "truth is stranger than fiction."

Just remember for a moment that he is the man to whom the shrewdest police, the sharpest detectives, and the most watchful jail wardens look with awe and anxiety.

And they are eminently right in this attitude of disquiet, because they know that buried in the brain of Houdini lies the secret of an unknown power he alone possesses that makes their prisons as powerless as Japanese screens, and renders their multiple-locking handcuffs, leg irons, and all the other prison paraphernalia, no more binding than store twine.

Suppose the innate and inherent integrity of character that Houdini possesses, in common with most men brought up within the circle of a mother's sweet influence, were to be swept aside by the desire for riches not his own. There are many men of many millions to-day whose money is not their own. Suppose he should be captured by a band of desperate men determined to wrest from Houdini this secret worth millions. Suppose a great hypnotist were to obtain dominance over this mystery-enveloped genius and use his baneful powers for evil designs. What then?

A slight knowledge of the marvels Houdini has accomplished mixed with a little imagination would create as many more suppositions of this kind as this book could contain.

But, to be brief, admitting the possibility of the happening of any of these suppositious instances, and you will gain a clear idea of the extraordinary character and quality of Houdini's powers. It is often the best way to see the full scope of a cause by carefully ascertaining its effect. This analytical method is equally applicable to Houdini, and recognizing the harm he would receive were his secrets confided to unworthy hands, you gain an adequately impressive idea of the enormity of responsibility that rests upon him.

Time and time again Houdini has encountered such perils, and in every case he owes his life and the preservation of his secret to his extraordinary acuteness of perception, to his marvelous knowledge of human nature, to his physical prowess that is far greater than appears from a merely superficial inspection, and, last and greatest of all, to the fact that the majority of people witnessing his wonders attribute a quasi supernatural power.

His press clipping books teems with stories proving the truth of one and all of these assertions. To glance over its pages enchains the reader's attention more closely that if he were absorbing an exciting romance. Accounts of thrilling jail-breaking feats are pasted beside stirring chronicling of handcuff escapes. Columns upon columns of laudatory press criticisms crowd colored cartoons and caricatures that connect Houdini and the great men of Europe in the great political crisis of the last few years.

It being true "that genius is but the capacity for hard work," then it is only a proper introductory tribute to Houdini to state that he is not a mushroomgrowth, sprouting and decaying in a night.

In the development and perfection of his astounding powers over metallic components Houdini has labored as tirelessly as Galileo constructing his astronomical theory, as Stephenson building the first locomotive, as Edison bringing to view the telephone, as Marconi revealing the wireless telegraph.

"How does he do it?" is the universal query.

Of course, he does not, he dare not tell what exertions of power, natural or supernatural, he makes in freeing himself from handcuffs, and in escaping from the dungeons that have held felons until the grave finally hid them forever.

Guesses are multiplied many, many times by all sorts and conditions of men and women. As many theories have been propounded as there are stars in the firmament. Some say he slips out of handcuffs like an eel slipping through an amateur fisherman's fingers. Others say he manipulates cell locks by muscular magnetism. A third class declares that he squeezes himself through bars of cells. Still more say spirits aid him in his escapes. And so, ad infitum.

Suffice it is to say that Houdini actually does all that the newspapers credit him doing.

He was born April 6th, 1874, in Appleton, Wis., and a little calculation will show that he is still far from the meridian of life. From the beginning he showed an insight into mechanics and mechanism that may be compared with the early endeavors of other men who have wrought wonders in the name of science. He showed a tendency toward travel, too, and in his ninth year had a brief experience with Jack Hoefler's "five cent" circus in his home town. Then came an apprenticeship as a mechanic, and after an uneventful term with "the tools of trade" Houdini resolved to see the great world with his own eager eyes. So he ran away from home, as so many others have done that in later years attributed their greatness to their early contact with the corrugated side of life. He joined a small circus, and, being exceptionally bright, he soon learned to conduct the Punch and Judy show, to do a ventriloquial act, and also to play clown on the bars. It may be, too, that "he doubled in brass" or played in the band, though he has never said so.

Here began the experiences that quickly ripened Houdini into the World's Handcuff King and Prison Breaker, which he is, has been and always will be. In exploring his wits for exploits to amuse and entertain the audiences, Houdini hit upon the feat of escaping from ropes tied round him in every conceivable way. He became so expert that he eventually offered a challenge of $25 to any one who could tie him so that he could not escape. And he never has lost a cent of the proffered money.

Then came the full turning-point in his career when he looked for greater worlds to conquer, and began the mastery of handcuffs, leg irons, shackles, etc. Of course, proficiency came with practice in secret, and then the public was permitted to witness the efforts of the young wizard.

Houdini went to England without an engagement. He went to Mr. Slater, manager of the Alhambra, London, gave several trial shows, got a contract for two weeks, then one for six months at £60 a week.

HOUDINI AT DIFFERENT AGES OF HIS CAREER

Since then he has been a top-of-the-bill star everywhere. He has made enormous salaries on the continent, where he is tremendously popular. He has broken records for paid admissions all over Continental Europe. In the week he performed before the Grand Duke of Russia he earned in public and private performances over £400, an enormous salary in those days.

In 1905, he returned to America for a brief tour, and he became at once the sensation in every city. Jails have fallen before his power like cities in the olden time before the armies of Caesar. The police of America join the gendarmerie of Europe in declaring, "Nothing on earth can hold him a prisoner." All the strongest cells and prisons in the United States have succumbed to the mysteriously potent force he exerts. Perhaps his most historic feat was his escape in January, 1906, from Cell 2, Condemned Murderers' Row, in the United States Jail at Washington, D. C., the very cell in which Guiteau, the assassin of President Garfield was confined until he was led forth to be hanged. Another great work was his escape from double confinements in the Boston Tombs at Boston, Mass. March 20, 1906.

Since 1908 Houdini has dropped handcuffs, and has made his performance replete with new mysteries, introducing his original invention—escaping out of an air-tight galvanized iron can filled with water, after it has been locked into an iron bound chest, and the intricate inexplicable escape from the Water Torture Cell, and releasing himself from a regulation strait jacket in full view of the audience, and during the week accepting various challenges.

Any reader of this who wishes to challenge Houdini, or has any novel method of securing Houdini, must write to publicly advertise address and name of Challenger or Challengers. No Challenge can be accepted for same date on which it is sent.

Instead of remaining in America six months as his original contract stipulated, he was the sensation of show business from his opening 1905, until his departure for Germany, August 1908.

NEW YORK
THE GREAT WHITE WAY

His leap from the Frederichstrasse Bridge, in Berlin, Germany, heavily manacled, September 5th, 1908; his daring plunge into the Weser, Bremen, having to break through ice, Paris, from the roof of the gruesome Morgue, April 7th, 1909, brought record houses at the Circus Busch, Berlin, and Alhambra Theatre, Paris, causing his imitators to try and duplicate his feats. Two were fortunately saved from a watery grave, Alburtus, in Atlantic City, being saved by the life-saving guard, Menkis was brought up in an unconscious state, and Ricardo jumped handcuffed from the Luippold Bridge, Landshut, Bavaria, April 14th, 1909, and was drowned.

Cold waters have no terrors for Houdini, as he dived manacled into the Mersey River, Liverpool, December 7th, 1908, also in the Egbaston Reservoir, Birmingham, December 15th, 1908. In all dives Houdini makes use of the regulation police handcuffs, chains, and leg irons.

Houdini returned to America again in 1914, just before the World War, toured the country, appearing for two seasons at the World's biggest Theatre, the New York Hippodrome, the first season presenting his inventions, The Vanishing Elephant, in which he caused an elephant named "Jennie" to vanish, who weighed over ten thousand pounds, and said to be a daughter of the beloved Barnum's "Jumbo," and in the second half of the Hippodrome show, performing the Submarine Box feat, escaping from same whilst under water, and the box being entirely filled with water.

Second season, introducing the Escape from Strait Jacket, suspended sixty feet in mid-air, hanging by his ankles, and presenting for the first time on any stage another of his inventions, The Whirlwind of Colors, in which he produced hundreds of yards of silks, giant flags, and for a finish the only tame American Eagle of this decade. It is known that Old Abe was a tame eagle, used by the Union soldiers as a mascot, but this Young Abe, trained by Houdini is the only one known that any one could handle.

Houdini gave his services to the Government, giving performances in the camps, for two consecutive years, not accepting engagements, and is proud of the fact of having sold over two million dollars worth of liberty bonds.

The years of 1918, 1920 and 1921 he became a Cinema star, recognizing the fact that Dame Nature would demand her due, and that the future generations would not believe that any man could perform the feats with which he is credited. So he originally went into a company to produce a 15 episode serial, "The Master Mystery," making such a sensational success that Mr. Jesse L. Lasky engaged him for a feature picture, "The Grim Game," and before this was released, Mr. Lasky re-engaged Houdini for a second picture, "Terror Island." Both features were the sensations of the year.

To fulfill contracts made eight years before Houdini, in January, 1920, returned to England for a tour of the principal music halls. So great was his success that even his former triumphs were eclipsed. Throngs followed him whenever he appeared on the streets of the provincial towns of Great Britain. He broke house record after house record, drawing such box office returns that the Moss Empires management waived its right to hold him to the figure named in the eight year old contract and voluntarily doubled his salary.

Upon his return to America Houdini organized his own film producing company of which more will be told in subsequent pages.

OFFICIAL POLICE NEWS FROM GERMANY!

HARRY HOUDINI, THE AMERICAN HANDCUFF KING, SUE.S THE COLOGNE POLICE FOR LIBEL, AND WINS!!!

A Condensed History of the Lawsuit Against the Cologne Police!

The police of Germany are very strict in matters of false billing or misrepresenting exhibitions to the public, and the case of the well-known Dr. Slade, also a well-known American "thaumaturgic" performer, as also an equally familiar "magnetic" woman, and several others who have clashed with the German police will probably also call in mind the latest case of the flower medium, Mrs. Rothe, who was sentenced to two years in prison and 500 marks fine.

What for? Well, she deceived the public in telling them that she could obtain communications from the spirit world.

This the police claim was obtaining money under false pretense, and there you are.

The Cologne police claimed that Houdini was also traveling about misrepresenting, and that all he did was "swindle." The chief one was Schutzmann Werner Graff, who openly published a false story in the *Rheinische Zeitung*, which put Houdini in a very bad light, and, as a man of honor, Houdini could not overlook the insult.

He claimed that he had been slandered, and asked an apology, also a retraction of the false stories, which all the press of Germany had copied; but was simply laughed at for his trouble.

Engaging the best lawyer of Cologne, Herr Rechtsantwalt Dr. Schreiber, Louisenstrasse 17, this able lawyer defended Houdini in all three instances.

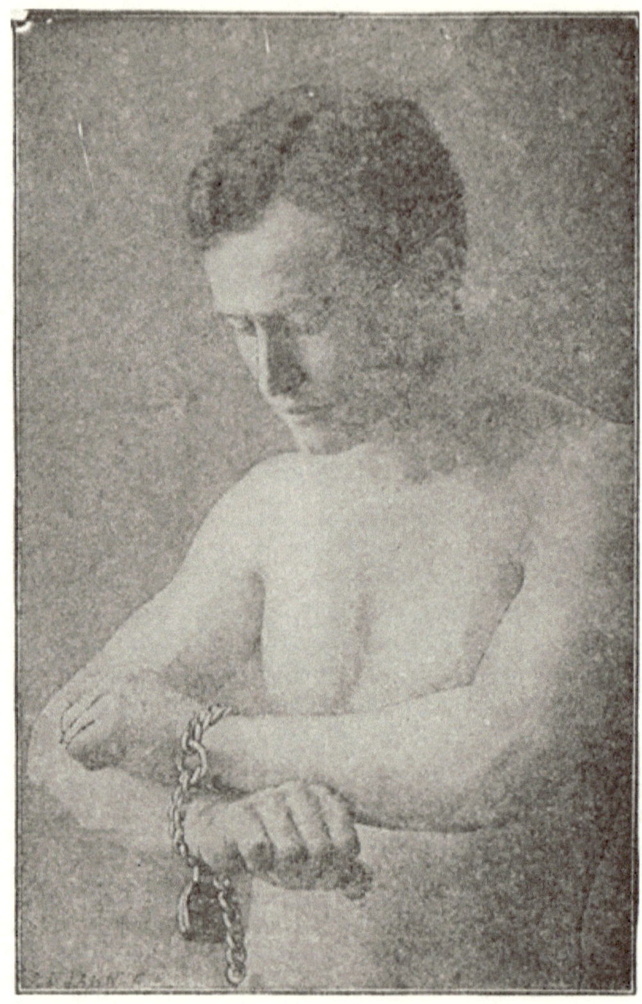

Houdini, as Chained and Handcuffed Before the Judges in the First Trial of His Action Against the Royal Police of Cologne.

The first trial occurred in Cologne, Feb. 19, 1902; in this trial Houdini charged the Schutzman Werner Graff for publicly slandering him, whereupon, as answer, Herr Graff told the judge and jury that he was willing to prove that Houdini was misrepresenting, that he could chain Houdini so that he could not release himself. Houdini permitted himself to be chained by Herr Transport Police Lott, and to show how easy it was he wilfully showed to the judge and jury how he opened the chain and lock.

After a four days' trial, Houdini won the lawsuit, and the Cologne police were fined, and were to publicly apologize to Houdini, "In the Name of the Kaiser."

Instead of so doing, they took it to the higher court, "Strafkammer." At this trial they had specially manufactured a lock, which was made by Master Mechanic Kroch, a lock that when once locked nothing would open it; even the key could not open the lock.

The police asked that Houdini should show his ability by opening this lock after it had once been locked.

The following is a free translation of what the press had to say at the second trial.

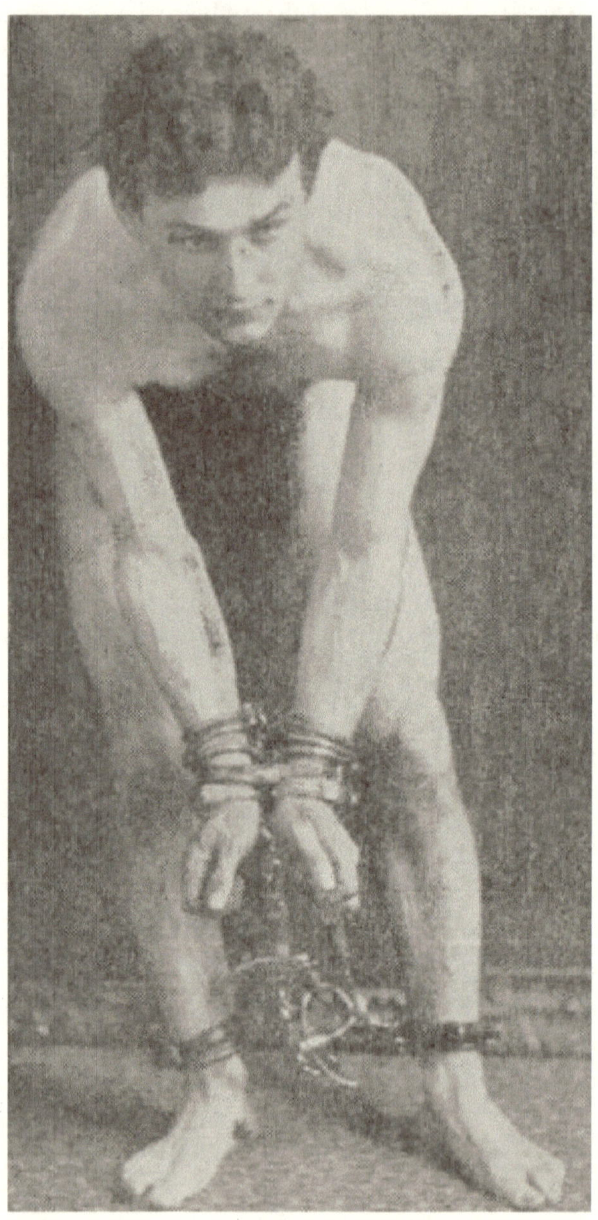

Houdini as Handcuffed and Manacled by the San Francisco Police, July, 1899.

In the highest court (Strafkammer zu Köln Yuli 26, 1902) Police Officer Werner Graff was found guilty of slandering Harry Houdini, heavily fined, he must pay all costs, and insert an advertisement in all of the Cologne newspapers, proclaiming his punishment, at the same time, "IN THE NAME OF THE KING," openly apologize to Houdini for insulting him.

This open apology is the severest punishment that can be given to a royal official, and as the lawsuit has been running over a year, the costs will run into the *thousands of marks*.

The case was first tried in the Schöffengericht Köln, Feb. 19, 1902, and Werner Graff was found guilty, but he took it to the highest court, and again Houdini won.

The Cologne police claimed that all Houdini advertised to do was misrepresentation (this was the cause of the lawsuit); for the trial they had a *special lock made that, after it was once locked, no key would open it.*

This lock they challenged Houdini to open, to prove that he was not misrepresenting.

Houdini accepts the challenge, walks into the room selected by the jury where he could work unhindered. In four minutes, with a quiet smile, reenters the court room, and hands the judges the prepared lock opened.

Among the thirty police officials that testified against Houdini were some of the highest officials of Cologne, but Houdini won; in fact, he was "one" too many for them.

**Houdini as Handcuffed and Manacled by the Dresden (Germany)
Police, September, 1900.**

Houdini as Handcuffed, Elbow-ironed, and Thumbscrewed by the Berlin Police, October, 1900.

It being a disgrace for Schutzman Werner Graff to have this punishment on him, with the assistance of the police, he took it to the highest court in Germany, "Oberlandesgericht," and there the learned judges again gave Houdini the verdict from which there is no appeal.

Below is a free translation of the apology as printed in the German papers:

IN THE NAME OF THE KING

BE it known that the artiste, known as HARRY HOUDINI, of America, New York City, against the Cologne Police Schutzman Werner Graff, for slandering (insulting).

The Demonstration Before the German Judiciary.

[Text in illustration: The Imperial Police of Cologne slanderously libeled HARRY HOUDINI, stating his advertised tricks were swindles!

HOUDINI answered them by sueing for "An Honorary Public Apology". The Police lost the Case in the three highest Courts, as they were unable to fetter or Chain HOUDINI in an unescapeable manner. He was even successful in opening a special lock that they had constructed which after it had once been locked could not be opened!

- First Trial "Königliches Schöffengericht" in Köln. Feb. 26 1902

- Second Trial "Königliche Strafkammer" in Köln. July 26 1902

- Third Trial "Königliches Oberlandesgericht". Sept. 26, 1902

Having lost the case in all three trials the Police were ultimately compelled to publicly advertise "An Honorary Apology" and pay all costs of the trials.

By command of Kaiser WILHELM II. Emperor of Germany.]

The Royal Schöffengericht, the third "Ferienstrafkammer," found Werner Graff guilty of slandering Houdini, and the Oberlandesgericht Court also find that the Royal Schöffengericht was justified in finding Graff guilty of the charges. Werner Graff is guilty of "Openly Slandering" Houdini, for being the chief instigator of the article which he caused to be inserted in the *Rheinische Zeitung* July 25, 1901, number of edition 170, and the head-lines which read "Houdini, the world-famous Handcuff Releaser." Being found guilty of the above charge, Werner Graff is fined 30 marks in money, and should he fail to pay the sum fine, he will serve a day in prison for every 5 marks; and is also fined to pay all costs of the three trials.

Houdini, as Handcuffed by the Vienna Police, March, 1902.

Houdini has the right to publish the verdict one time in the Cologne newspapers at the cost of Schutzman Werner Graff.

For the rightful writing of this verdict, we sign as responsibilities, Coln, Oct. 24, 1902. Stock Sekretar.

Gerichtsschreiber des Kgl. Amtsgericht Abtlg VI.—9.

Signed for Houdini,

Rechtsanwalt Dr. Schreiber Köln.

It will be of interest to note that Houdini has escaped out of prisons and cells in the following cities:

New York, W. 125th Street Police Station, W. 68th Street Police Station, and W. 37th Street; Brooklyn, N. Y.; Newark, N. J.; Salem, Mass.; Lowell, Mass.; Rochester, N. Y.; Baltimore; Washington (3 different places); Detroit, Mich.; Philadelphia, Pa.; Providence, R. I.; Kansas City; Buffalo, N. Y.; and Chicago, Ill.; Amsterdam, Hague; Dordrecht, Holland; Moscow, Russia; Halifax; Bradford; Leicester; Burnley; Leeds; Newcastle-upon-Tyne; Sheffield; Liverpool; South Shields; Salford; Huddersfield; Manchester; St. Helens; Stockton-on-Tees; Eastbourne; Newport, Mon.

Space prohibits the publication of all certificates from the various chiefs of police, but a few are selected, which follow:

Chief Constable's Office,

Sheffield, Jan. 19, 1904.

This is to certify that Mr. Harry Houdini was this day stripped stark naked and locked in the cell which once contained Charles Peace. The cell was searched and triple-locked, but Mr. Houdini released himself and redressed in five minutes, having also opened the iron gate of the corridor.

Charles J. Scott, Commander (R.N.)

Chief Constable, Sheffield.

Witness to the foregoing feat,

George H. Barker, Deputy Chief Constable.

An exceedingly rare photograph of Charles Peace, shrewdest, most dangerous and notorious criminal in the annals of Crime in Great Britain. Peace broke jail a number of times but failed to escape from this cell in Sheffield. He was hanged at the Armley jail. Houdini escaped from this cell, as Chief Constable Scott's certificate on page 12 shows.

May 10, 1903.

Harry Houdini was made to disrobe, and in a nude condition was locked into the Moscow transportation cell or carette, and in less than 20 minutes he had managed to make his escape. The searching Houdini had to submit to in the hands of the secret Russian police was the severest he has ever had to undergo. Never in the history of the Russian police has any one been able to escape out of this or any other transportation carette. This feat was accomplished in the presence of Chief of the Secret Police Cos, Lebadeff.

Houdini was booked for one month in Moscow, but after this feat he was prolonged for four months, and proved the greatest sensation that ever visited Russia.

From the German police Houdini possesses certificates from the cities of Berlin, Dresden, Dusseldorf, Essen Ruhr, Barmen, Bremen, Dortmund, Leipzig, Frankfort A/M, Hanover, etc.; but the following is the principal one:

ROYAL POLICE PRESIDIUM,

BERLIN, Sept. 20, 1900.

Harry Houdini, the American, was handcuffed and leg-ironed with the irons used here, in the presence of a large number of the highest police officials of Germany. Houdini managed to free himself from everything, by mysteriously opening the locks, in a manner which is unexplainable to us. The cuffs were uninjured.

(Signed) VON HULLESSEM, Royal Police Director, Berlin.

VON WINDHEIM, The Royal Police President, Berlin.

Von Windheim was the highest police official in all Germany. The Kaiser's signature was the only name that stood higher in Germany.

The Preparation for Incarceration in the Siberian Transport Carette.

[Text in illustration: Chief of the Secret Russian Police LEBEDOEFF has HARRY HOUDINI stripped stark naked and searched then locked up in the Siberian Transport Cell or Carette, May 10/1903 in Moscow and in 28 minutes HOUDINI had made his escape to the unspeakable astonishment of the Russian Police.]

The Daily Illustrated Mirror, March 18th, 1904.

HOW HE PICKED THE "MIRROR" HAND-CUFFS IN ONE HOUR AND TEN MINUTES.

Not a seat was vacant in the mighty Hippodrome, yesterday afternoon, when Harry Houdini, the "Handcuff King," stepped into the arena, and received an ovation worthy of a monarch.

For days past all London has been aware that on Saturday night last a representative of the *Mirror* had stepped into the arena, in response to Houdini's challenge to anybody to come forward and successfully manacle him, and had there and then made a match with America's Mysteriarch for Thursday afternoon.

In his travels the journalist had encountered a Birmingham blacksmith who had spent five years of his life in devising a lock, which, he alleged, "no mortal man could pick." Promptly seeing he was in touch with a good thing, the press man had at once put an option upon the handcuff containing this lock, and brought it back to London with him.

It was submitted to London's best locksmiths, who were unanimous in their admiration of it, asserting that in all their experience they had never before seen such wonderful mechanism.

As a result the editors of the *Mirror* determined to put the lock to the severest test possible by challenging Mr. Houdini to be manacled with the cuffs.

Like a true sportsman, Mr. Houdini accepted our challenge in the spirit in which it was given, although, on his own confession, he did not like the look of the lock.

MIGHTY AUDIENCE.

Mr. Houdini's call was for three o'clock yesterday, but so intense was the excitement that the 4,000 spectators present could scarcely restrain their impatience whilst the six excellent turns which preceded him, cheered to the echo on other occasions, got through their "business."

Waiting quietly and unnoticed by the arena steps, the *Mirror* representative watched Mr. Houdini's entrance, and joined in giving his opponent-to-be in the lists one of the finest ovations mortal man has ever received.

"I am ready," said Houdini, concluding his address to the audience, "to be manacled by the *Mirror* representative if he be present."

A hearty burst of applause greeted the journalist as he stepped into the arena and shook hands with the "Handcuff King."

Then, in the fewest possible words, the press man called for volunteers from the audience to act upon a committee to see fair play, and Mr. Houdini asked his friends also to step into the arena and watch his interests.

HOUDINI HANDCUFFED.

This done, the journalist placed the handcuffs on Mr. Houdini's wrists and snapped them. Then, with an effort, he turned the key six times, thus securing the bolt as firmly as possible.

The committee being satisfied as to the security of the handcuff, Mr. Houdini said:—

"*Ladies and Gentlemen*:—I am now locked up in a handcuff that has taken a British mechanic five years to make. I do not know whether I am going to get out of it or not, but I can assure you I am going to do my best."

Applauded to the echo, the Mysteriarch then retired within the cabinet that contains so many of his secrets.

All correct chronometers chronicled 3.15.

In a long line in front of the stage stood the committee. Before them, in the center of the arena, stood the little cabinet Houdini loves to call his "ghost house." Restlessly pacing to and fro, the *Mirror* representative kept an anxious eye on it.

FALSE HOPE OVERTHROWN.

Those who have never stood in the position of a challenger can scarcely realize the sense of responsibility felt by one who has openly thrown down the gauntlet to a man who is popular with the public.

The *Mirror* had placed its reliance on the work of a British mechanic, and if Houdini succeeded in escaping in the first few minutes it was felt that the proceedings would develop into a mere farce.

But time went by; 5, 10, 15, 20 minutes sped. Still the band played on. Then, at 22 minutes, Mr. Houdini put his head out of the "ghost house," and this was the signal for a great outburst of cheering.

"He is free! he is free!" shouted several; and universal disappointment was felt when it was ascertained that he had only put his head outside the cabinet in order to get a good look at the lock in strong electric light.

From a Photo of the Famous Scene in the London, England, Hippodrome, when Houdini was Handcuffed by the London Illustrated Mirror Representative.

The band broke into a dreamy waltz as Houdini once more disappeared within the canopy. The disappointed spectators looked at their watches, murmured "What a shame!" gave Houdini an encouraging clap, and the journalist resumed his stride.

At 35 minutes Mr. Houdini again emerged. His collar was broken, water trickled in great channels down his face, and he looked generally warm and uncomfortable.

"My knees hurt," he explained to the audience. "I am not done yet."

The "house" went frantic with delight at their favorite's resolve, and this suggested an idea to the *Mirror* representative.

He spoke rapidly to Mr. Parker, the Hippodrome manager, who was at the side of the stalls. That gentleman looked thoughtful for a moment, then nodded his head and whispered something to an attendant.

A WELCOME CONCESSION.

Presently the man appeared bearing a large cushion.

"The *Mirror* has no desire to submit Mr. Houdini to a torture test," said the representative; "and if Mr. Houdini will permit me, I shall have great pleasure in offering him the use of this cushion."

The "Handcuff King" was glad evidently of the rest for his knees, for he pulled it through into the "ghost house."

Ladies trembled with suppressed excitement, and, despite the weary wait, not a yawn was noticed throughout the vast audience. For 20 minutes more the band played on, and then Houdini was seen to emerge once more from the cabinet.

Still handcuffed!

Almost a moan broke over the vast assemblage as this was noticed. He looked in pitiable plight from his exertions and much exhausted.

He looked about for a moment, and then advanced to where his challenger stood.

"Will you remove the handcuffs for a moment," he said, "in order that I may take my coat off?"

For a few seconds the journalist considered. Then he replied: "I am indeed sorry to disoblige you, Mr. Houdini, but I cannot unlock those cuffs unless you admit you are defeated."

The reason was obvious. Mr. Houdini had seen the cuffs locked, but he had never seen them unlocked. Consequently the press man thought there might be more in the request than appeared on the surface.

FROCK COAT SACRIFICED.

Houdini evidently does not stick at trifles. He maneuvered until he got a penknife from his waistcoat pocket. This he opened with his teeth, and then, turning his coat inside out over his head, calmly proceeded to cut it to pieces.

The novelty of the proceeding delighted the audience, who yelled themselves frantic. The *Mirror* representative had rather a warm five minutes of it at this juncture. Many of the audience did not see the reason of his refusal, and expressed their disapproval of his action loudly.

Grimly, however, he looked on and watched Mr. Houdini once more reenter the cabinet. Time sped on, and presently somebody recorded the fact that the Mysteriarch had been manacled just one hour. Ten minutes more of anxious waiting, and then a surprise was in store for everybody.

VICTORY.

The band was just finishing a stirring march when, with a great shout of victory, Houdini bounded from the cabinet, holding the shining handcuffs in his hand—free!

A mighty roar of gladness went up. Men waved their hats, shook hands one with the other. Ladies waved their handkerchiefs, and the committee, rushing forward as one man, shouldered Houdini, and bore him in triumph round the arena.

But the strain had been too much for the "Handcuff King," and he sobbed as though his heart would break.

With a mighty effort, however, he regained his composure, and received the congratulations of the *Mirror* in the true sportsmanlike spirit he has shown throughout the contest.

PRESENTATION MODEL

The journalist intimated to the audience that a beautiful solid silver model of the handcuffs would be made, and asked Mr. Houdini's permission to present this to him at no distant date.

A SPORTSMAN'S TELEGRAM.

Late last night Mr. Houdini sent us the following telegram:

Editor "Mirror," 2, Carmelite Street, London. E. C.

"Allow me to thank you for the open and upright manner in which your representative treated me in to-day's contest. Must say that it was one of the hardest, but at the same time one of the fairest tests I ever had."

"HARRY HOUDINI."

HOUDINI, manacled and chained, Diving head first off Queen's Bridge, into the Yarra River, Melbourne, Australia, Feb. 18th, 1910.

Australia's Coast is infested with Man-eating Sharks, luckily for Houdini, none happened to be around when he dived.

AN EPISODE IN HOUDINI'S LIFE.

Star, Blackburn, England, Saturday, Oct. 25, 1902.

MANACLED BY A STRONG MAN.
TRUSSED TILL MIDNIGHT.

Unparalleled Scenes at the Palace Theatre.

Never in the history of Blackburn or music hall life has there been witnessed so remarkable a scene as occurred last night. Houdini, the Handcuff King, and Mr. Hodgson, principal of the School of Physical Culture, provided a big sensation for the patrons of the Palace Theatre, Blackburn.

Houdini, who has been appearing at the Palace during the week, claims to be able to release himself from any of the regulation shackles or irons used by the police of Europe or America, and offered nightly to forfeit £25 if he failed to prove his claim.

Mr. Hodgson, of the Physical Culture School, Blackburn, took up the challenge, stipulating that he was to use his own irons and fix them himself. Houdini consented, and deposited the £25 with the editor of the *Daily Star*.

The trial of skill and strength was fixed to take place last night, and the crowd which came together to witness it crammed the theatre literally from floor to ceiling—even standing room being ultimately unobtainable.

Shortly after ten o'clock the parties to the challenge faced each other, and excitement at once became intense.

Mr. Hodgson produced 6 pairs of heavy irons, furnished with clanking chains and swinging padlocks. These were carefully examined by Houdini, who raised some disappointment and much sympathetic cheering by stating that his claim was that he could escape from "regulation" irons. The "cuffs" brought by Mr. Hodgson, he said, had been tampered with—the iron being wrapped round with string, the locks altered, and various other expedients adopted to render escape more difficult.

Mr. Hodgson's answer, given dramatically from the stage, was that he stipulated that he should bring his own irons.

Houdini again protested that Mr. Hodgson was going beyond the challenge, but added that he was quite willing to go on, if only the audience would give him a little time in which to deal with the extra difficulties.

This announcement was greeted with great cheering, and the work of pinioning proceeded.

First, Mr. Hodgson, with the aid of a companion, fixed a pair of irons over Houdini's upper arm, passing the chain behind his back and pulling it tight, and fixing the elbows close to the sides.

To make assurance doubly sure, he fixed another pair in the same way, and padlocked both behind.

Then, starting with the wrists, he fixed a pair of chained "cuffs" so that the arms, already pulled stiffly behind, were now pulled forward. The pulling and tugging at this stage was so severe—the strong man exercising his strength to some purpose—that Houdini protested that it was no part of the challenge that his arms should be broken.

He also reminded Mr. Hodgson that he was to fix the irons himself.

This led to Mr. Hodgson's assistant retiring.

Proceeding, Mr. Hodgson fixed a second pair of "cuffs" on the wrists and padlocked both securely, Houdini's arms being then trussed to his side so securely that escape seemed absolutely impossible.

Still Mr. Hodgson was not finished with him.

Getting Houdini to kneel down, he passed the chain of a pair of heavy leg irons through the chains which bound the arms together at the back. These were fixed to the ankles, and after a second pair had been added, both were locked, and Houdini now seemed absolutely helpless.

A canopy being placed over Houdini in the middle of the stage, the waiting began, and excitement grew visibly every minute.

Meanwhile Mr. Hodgson and others kept strict watch on the movements of Houdini's wife and brother (Hardeen), who were both on the stage.

At the end of about 15 minutes the canopy was lifted and Houdini was revealed lying on his side, still securely bound. It was at first thought he had fainted, but he soon made it known that all he wished was to be lifted up. This Mr. Hodgson refused to do, at which the now madly excited audience hissed and "booed" him for his unfair treatment, and Hardeen lifted his brother to his knees. The curtain of the cabinet was again closed.

Another 20 minutes passed, and again the curtain was lifted. This time Houdini said his arms were bloodless and numb owing to the pressure of the irons, and asked to have them unlocked for a minute so that the circulation could be restored.

Mr. Hodgson's reply, given amidst howls, was: "This is a contest, not a love match. If you are beaten, give in."

Great shouting and excited calling followed, which was renewed when Dr. Bradley, after examining Houdini, said his arms were blue, and it was cruelty to keep him chained up as he was any longer.

Still Mr. Hodgson was obdurate, and the struggle proceeded, Houdini again appealing for time.

Fifteen minutes more: Houdini appeared and announced that one hand was free.

This was the signal for terrific cheering, which was continued after the canopy was dropped.

At intervals Houdini now appeared, and announced further progress in his escape; and when, shortly after midnight, he came out with torn clothing and bleeding arms, and threw the last of the shackles on the stage, the vast audience stood up and cheered and cheered, and yelled themselves hoarse to give vent to their overwrought feelings. Men and women hugged each other in mad excitement. Hats, coats, and umbrellas were thrown up into the air, and pandemonium reigned supreme for 15 minutes.

Houdini, when quietness had been restored, said he had been doing the hand-cuff trick now for 14 years, but never had he been subjected to such brutality as that to which his bleeding arms and wrists gave witness.

When Houdini again obtained a hearing, it was to state that, not only had the irons been altered, but the locks had been plugged.

It was well after midnight when the huge audience left the theatre, and broke up into excited, gesticulating groups.

CONDEMNED MURDERERS RELEASED BY HOUDINI.

The Washington Post, Sunday, Jan. 7, 1906.

OUT OF GUITEAU CELL.

HOUDINI MIXES THINGS UP AT THE UNITED STATES JAIL. PRISONERS CHANGED IN CELLS.

Consternation Accompanies Feats of the Expert Lock-picker, Who Gets Laurels from the American Police Chairman After His Third Exploit in Washington—Crowds Are Transfixed.

Two condemned murderers, four others under indictment, and two noted criminals were released from the United States jail yesterday and for a brief time tasted a counterfeit liberty.

Harry Houdini, the international Prison Breaker and Handcuff King, as he is styled, was the hero of a sensational exploit. On the invitation of Warden Harris and the jail authorities he ravaged bolts and locks.

Houdini escaped from the cell in which Charles J. Guiteau, the assassin of President Garfield, was confined, released all the other inmates of the murderers' row cells, and transferred each into some other cell than the one to which he was originally committed.

For several days—in fact, since Houdini's remarkable escape from the Tenth precinct—Warden Harris, of the cathedral-like prison along the Eastern Branch of the Potomac, has been endeavoring to secure Houdini for a cell-breaking exploit, as the warden had full faith in the efficiency of his lock system. He wished to have this faith justified by an attempt at escape of Houdini, and his failure would induce that state of mind.

JAMES A. GARFIELD
the Martyred President

Copyright and Published by J. F. RYDER, Cleveland, O.
The sitting for this portrait was made June 10th, 1880

Until yesterday Houdini has been so occupied with his other invitations to break out of the police cells and the other penal institutions that he had abandoned the idea of an adventure at the jail. Not wishing to seem discourteous, he concluded about noon yesterday to present his compliments to Warden Harris and assure him that he would be pleased to test the jail.

CROWD QUICKLY GATHERS

The news of his presence traveled the length of the offices on the inside of the big structure, and here there gathered in the warden's office the following officials and visitors: Deputy Warden W. Grayson Urner, Capt. Ed. S. Randell, Guards John C. Campbell, George C. Gumm, James Corrigan, and John P. Hickey, Jail Physician Dr. D. Kerfoot Shute, Dr. H. I. Sout, Dr. T. Sullivan, Clerk J. Fred Harris, and Messrs. Robert R. Mahorney, Theo Judd, Frank Jones, David M. Proctor, and John T. Ward.

Houdini was invited to examine the cell arrangement and was shown first to Murderers' Row, which is in the south wing and comprises seventeen cells, containing Walter H. Hamilton, sentenced to be hanged last November, but now living through stayed proceedings; Richard Chase, sentenced to twelve years for manslaughter; Thomas S. Whitney, John Mercer, Edward Ferguson, Jeremiah Donovan, and Henry Gaskins—these having been indicted for murder, their alleged crimes being still fresh in the public mind; also James A. Backus, the alleged money-order raiser, and Clarence Howlett, sentenced for housebreaking.

Entered according to act of Congress, in the year 1881, by
C. M. BELL
in the office of the Librarian of Congress, at Washington, D. C.

GUITEAU, the assassin of President Garfield. Houdini escaped from the murderer's cell in which this assassin was secured.

Houdini was chiefly interested in cell No. 2, the one occupied by Guiteau, and presumably the safest of the lot, although it was from the outside of this cell that "Avenger" Jones shot into it in his effort to kill the assassin. It now holds Hamilton, who is alleged to have smothered his wife to death and then sat all night beside the body of his victim, indulging in a drunken orgy. The officials say that he is one of the most orderly prisoners ever out there. Howard Schneider, who murdered his wife and her brother, and Shæfer, the murderer hanged a short time ago, also occupied this cell.

PONDEROUS BARRED DOORS.

All these cells are brick structures with their doors sunk into the walls fully three feet from the face of the outer corridor wall. When the heavily barred door is closed, an armlike bar runs out to the corridor wall and then angles to the right and slips over a steel catch which sets a spring that fastens the lock. The latter is only opened by a key, and there are no less than five tumblers in the lock. One key opens all the doors in the corridor.

With Houdini there, it was very natural that everybody should express the ardent desire to have him then and there go into a cell and see if he could release himself, and Houdini, with his accustomed courtesy, yielded a ready acquiescence. He insisted, however, that he preferred to try cell No. 2, for the reason that it is the hardest one there to get out of alive, as he expressed it, and because of the notorious murderers who have spent their last moments on earth within its whitewashed walls.

This was agreed upon, and then he was stripped to the skin and locked into No. 2 with Hamilton, the negro, who crouched in the far corner of the cell, presumably laboring under the belief that one of the arch-fiends was already there to get him for a red-hot furnace. In two minutes Houdini was out of that cell, free, the lock holding him hardly longer than it took him to get into the place and get his bearings. Then, without the knowledge of the waiting officials who had retired from view, Houdini quickly ran to the cells of Chase, Whitney, Mercer, Ferguson, Donovan, Gaskins, Backus, and Howlett. To each occupant the unclad cell-breaker seemed like an apparition from some other world, and the astonishment he created when he commanded each to come out and follow him can be better imagined than described.

PRISONERS ARE DUMBFOUNDED

Chase gave a gasp of fear, and then cried, "Have you come to let me out? What are you doing without clothes?" He supposed then that Houdini was an escaping fellow-prisoner. He followed at Houdini's heels and the cell-breaker dashed with him down to the end of the corridor, where he opened the cell containing Clarence Howlett.

"What are you doing here?" said Houdini to the astonished Howlett. "What are you in for?"

"I'm a housebreaker," said the prisoner, as though making his last confession.

"You're a bad one," said Houdini, "or you could get out of here. Come along." Howlett followed his strange captor, and Houdini then thrust Chase into the cell and rushed Howlett up to Chase's cell.

This scene, strange and strenuous, was repeated again and again, until every desperate man was changed into another cell than his own. All were in a tumult. Twenty-one minutes after Houdini had been locked in the cell he had done all the quick changing and stood before his free audience in the main hall, clothed as in every-day manner.

When the officials found what he had done with their prisoners, their amazement passed all bounds. They took the slight change Houdini made in their plans with the utmost good nature, and soon had everything straightened out, and each of the men back in his cell. At the conclusion, Warden Harris gave the cell-breaker a certificate, of which the following is a copy:

"This is to certify that Mr. Harry Houdini, at the United States jail to-day, was stripped stark naked, thoroughly searched, and locked up in cell No. 2 of the south wing, the cell in which Charles J. Guiteau was confined from the date of his commitment, July 2, 1881, until the day on which he was executed, June 30, 1882. Mr. Houdini, in about 2 minutes, managed to escape from that cell, and then broke into the cell in which his clothing was locked up. He then proceeded to release from their cells all the prisoners on the ground floor. There was positively no chance for any collusion or confederacy. Mr. Houdini accomplished all of the above-mentioned feats, in addition to putting on all his clothing, in 21 minutes.

"J. H. HARRIS.

"Warden United States Jail, D. C."

Major Sylvester yesterday prepared for Houdini the following statement:

TO WHOM IT MAY CONCERN: No individual should be disinclined to profit by the abilities displayed by others, and, in order that defective means of restraint might be discovered in the holding of prisoners in this jurisdiction, and with a view to remedying any insecurity which might exist, Mr. Houdini, the expert man with locks, was permitted to examine a modern cell lock and attachment, and then placed in an entirely different cell from the one he examined. He was searched, and in a nude condition placed behind the bars, and, as supposed, secured. This was in the presence of the Engineer Officer of the District of Columbia, myself, and several officers. In 26 minutes he emerged from the cell and corridor fully attired.

"The experiment was a very valuable one in that the department has been instructed as to the adoption of further security which will protect any lock from being opened or interfered with. The act was interesting and profitable, and worthy of study.

"Mr. Houdini impressed his audience as a gentleman and an artist who does not profess to do the impossible.

"RICHARD SYLVESTER,

"Major and Superintendent."

SOME OF THE GREAT FEATS ACCOM-PLISHED BY HOUDINI.

Broke out of the Siberian Prison Van in Moscow, Russia, in May, 1903.

Leaped, heavily handcuffed, in zero weather, from Belle Island Bridge, in Detroit, Mich., in December 2nd, 1906, and released himself under the icy water.

Leaped into San Francisco Bay, San Francisco, Calif., on August 26th, 1907, handcuffed with hands behind his back, with more than 75 pounds of ball and chain locked to his body.

Escaped from a plate glass box made by the Pittsburg Plate Glass Co., and did not even scratch the glass. Boston Mass., Jan. 20th 1907.

After being rivetted into a large hot water boiler by the employees of the Marine Boiler Works, of Toledo, on March 15th, 1907, Houdini escaped without leaving any traces of his exit.

The biggest-little mystery feat—the East Indian needle masterpiece,

wherein Houdini swallows 100 needles, 20 yards of thread, and brings up the needles threaded.

Escaped from paper bags, zinc lined piano boxes, packing cases, padded cells, straight-jackets, insane cribs, willow hampers, iron cages, a U.S. Mail Pouch furnished with a rotary lock belonging to the U.S. Government, a large Football, made by Reach Company, of Philadelphia, a large Derby Desk, with secret locks, Burglar-proof safes, etc., etc. Handcuffed nailed into a packing case, 200 lbs. of iron weights chained to the box and was then thrown overboard into New York Bay.

Houdini has escaped from cells in almost every city in America, the most notable one being from the Murderers' Cell in U.S. Jail at Washington, D.C., which confined Guiteau, the murderer of President Garfield.

Houdini presents the largest, the smallest and most perplexing mystery in the world and history of magic.

The smallest. The East Indian Needle Mystery, in which he swallows 50 to 100 needles, 20 yards of thread, and brings them all up threaded, after his mouth and throat have been examined by a committee of Surgeons. In Boston, at Keith's Theatre, 1906, at special morning performance, he performed this feat before sixteen hundred physicians, and not one could give a correct solution as to his method.

The largest and one of his original inventions being the complete vanishing of a Ten Thousand pound Elephant, in full glare of the light and right over the tank of a Quarter of a Million Gallons of Water on the stage of New York Hippodrome, 1916-1917. He performed this the entire season, creating the greatest amount of talk ever caused by any Illusionist with any vanishing mystery.

The greatest mystery ever presented, original inventions of Houdini, one of the Chinese Torture Cell, and the Escape from a Packing Case which being weighted with 300 lbs. of pig iron is thrown overboard into the ocean, and from which he releases himself in less than two minutes.

Kansas City, Mo., April 11, 1900.

TO WHOM IT MAY CONCERN: We, the undersigned, do hereby certify that we saw Harry Houdini stripped nude, thoroughly searched from head to foot, and his mouth sealed up, making it an utter impossibility for him to have anything concealed on his person. We saw him handcuffed and leg-ironed with five different cuffs, and his hands locked to his feet.

He was led into a cell, which was also securely locked with what is known as the three-bond lock, guaranteed by the makers to be burglar proof. Nevertheless, Houdini succeeded in making his escape out of all the irons, also from the cell, in less than 8 minutes. There was no possible chance of confederacy.

Signed and sealed by JOHN HAYES, Chief of Police.

JOHN HALPIN, Inspector of Detectives.

J. C. SNAVLY, Jailer.

THE DISAPPEARING ELEPHANT
THE LARGEST VANISH THE WORLD HAS EVER KNOWN,
AS INVENTED AND PRESENTED BY HOUDINI AT THE NEW
YORK HIPPODROME.

Daily Express, London, Feb. 3, 1904.

WIZARD IN GAOL.

OPENS CELLS AND IS TAKEN FOR THE DEVIL.

HIS 61st ESCAPE.

I certify that to-day Mr. Harry Houdini showed his abilities in releasing himself from restraint.

He had three pairs of handcuffs, one a very close-fitting pair, placed round his wrists, and he was placed in a nude state in a cell which had been previously searched. Within 6 minutes he was free from the handcuffs, had opened the cell door, and had opened the doors of all the other cells in the corridor, had changed a prisoner from one cell to another, and had so securely locked him in that he had to be asked to unlock the door.

(Signed) LEONARD DUNNING,

Head Constable, Liverpool.

Feb. 2, 1902.

Mr. Dunning has since been knighted and is now head of the Police Constabulary, being located in London, his official title being His Majesty's Inspector of Constabulary, London, England.

For him it is literally true that—

Stone walls do not a prison make,
Nor iron bars a cage.

Were he a criminal—his clear, straightforward eyes negative the suggestion—he would be a nightmare to the police of Britain, for he would walk out of gaol as coolly and smilingly as he did twice out of Liverpool Bridewell yesterday.

It was an eventful day at the sinister-looking building that stands off busy Dale Street.

High police officials, clever detectives, leading city business men who hold office on the watch committee, all sustained a severe shock by their loss of faith in what they had regarded as an inviolable stronghold.

No one has been known previously to escape from the bolts and bars behind which Liverpool quarters its criminals.

SURRENDERS TO POLICE.

In the afternoon Houdini had a pleasant interview with Head Constable Dunning.

"Want to try our locks? Certainly. You're welcome; but, of course, we will take some precautions."

"I want you to do so," replied Houdini. "I will strip naked. You can then handcuff me and put me in your strongest cell, and after you have searched me and the cell you leave me, locking the door. I will join you in a minute or two."

Houdini was as good as his word. Not only did he escape, but he had torn from his hands and arms three pairs of handcuffs, which had been put on him by officers with absolute belief in their restraining power.

Even these feats were not enough for this man, who does things that would have made Jack Sheppard die of envy. He felt sure there was nothing in Bridewell to baffle him.

Running along the corridor, he opened the doors of other cells, which he had thought were all empty. When he reached No. 14 and flung open the door, he confronted a prisoner.

"I don't know which of us was the more surprised," said Houdini to an *Express* representative.

STARTLED PRISONER

Here was I, standing absolutely nude before a terrified, miserable object.

Poor fellow! what a shock it was for him. He was an Irishman just recovering from a drunken bout.

"'Arrah!' he said, when he had recovered; 'I thought it was the divil.'"

The shivering prison-breaker hurried the wretched prisoner out of cell No. 14 into No. 15 and locked him in. Then he ran along the passage to greet the head constable and the other officials.

Only 6 minutes had elapsed since he had been locked in the cell naked and handcuffed. The cell door was inspected and found uninjured.

Then one of the gaolers, walking along the corridor, espied door No. 14 open and a prisoner gone.

"That's all right," said the irrepressible Houdini. "I've had him out and locked him up in No. 15." Hearty laughter followed the narration of this achievement, and the officials went to No. 15.

So securely had the Irishman been locked up that it was necessary to call upon Houdini to unfasten the door. The Irishman was found in a somewhat bewildered state, but he probably "sobered" quicker than he would have done in less eventful circumstances.

Houdini left the bridewell the proud possessor of the certificate which is re-produced at the head of this article.

ANOTHER EXPERIMENT

In the evening Houdini, accompanied by an Express representative, again walked into the bridewell to settle a point which had been raised since his feat in the afternoon.

Was the door which had been fastened against him single, double, or triple locked?

The matter could easily be settled. Houdini would just do the trick again. Only this time he would do it with his clothes on, as time was pressing.

Liverpool's bridewell is as an unsightly a place as a bridewell can be. No one would mistake it for a spa hotel or a convalescent home.

Beneath a dark arch you pass, and in the great door which you find opposite is a little window which is unlocked when you knock, and through which you are viewed before you are permitted even to stand upon the threshold.

Houdini and his companion were admitted.

"More lock-breaking?

"Yes; I am ready for more—as many as you like."

Accompanied by a gaoler, Houdini and the **Express** representative ascended a flight of stone steps and passed along dimly lighted corridors, whose atmosphere seemed to reek with crime and mystery.

Passing through a gate, a row of cells was reached, upon any one of which Houdini might operate.

Here was one marked with a strange device. Houdini would try this one.

It was a felon's cell—stronger than some of the others, though it could not have been darker or more forbidding.

Houdini entered. He was backed in by the **Express** representative. He was inside, safe and sound.

SECOND ESCAPE

There could be no doubt about that. At the first turn of the key the lock went forward twice; at the second, once. Houdini was behind a triple lock in the dark, dreary cell.

The **Express** representative and the gaoler left him there, and retired beyond an iron gate which bars the passage.

"The gate is a greater test than the cell," said the gaoler.

"It's locked before it's locked, if you understand. Shut it, and it's locked, and then you can lock it again."

The gaoler hand only secured it when Houdini presented himself.

"That's as quick as I've ever done it," said he. And then he tackled the gate.

A moment's hesitation. The gaoler shook his head, and a smile was just over-spreading his features, when lo! Houdini flung open wide the gate.

He agreed that the gate was "tougher," as he expressed it, than the cell.

Houdini is an American. Only his strong arms and his supple, yet powerful hands give the slightest clue of his prison-breaking capacity.

He does not look a gaolbird, but the escape he made for the benefit of **Express** readers was his 61st.

Bright-eyed, smart, active, and a good talker, he has traveled far and wide, and has broken out of the prisons of many countries.

"I have never failed," said Houdini, "but I don't say there is no cell I cannot break out of. As to handcuffs, the hardest job I ever had was with a pair made at Krupp's. It took me 40 minutes to get out of them, but I did it."

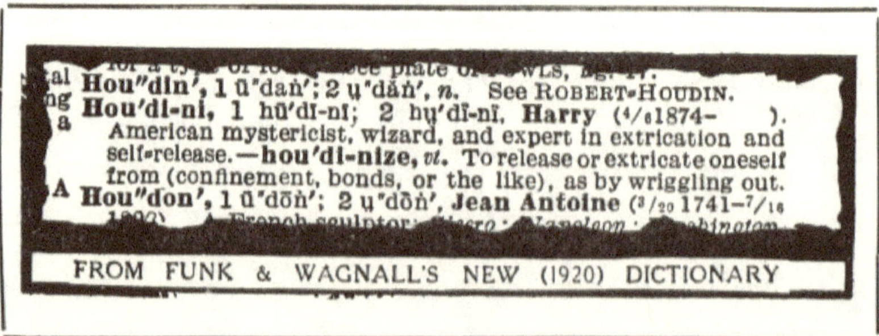

Hou'di-ni, 1 hū'dĭ-nĭ; 2 hu'dĭ-nĭ, Harry (4/6 1874-). American mys-tericist, wizard, and expert in extrication and self-release.—hou'di-nize, _vt._ To release or extricate oneself from (confinement, bonds, or the like), as by wriggling out.

FROM FUNK & WAGNALL'S NEW (1920) DICTIONARY

HOUDINI OUTWITS FIJI ISLANDER SWIMMING CHAMPION.

Houdini, the man of mystery, who is now appearing in our midst, is certainly a peculiar species of a human being. From all accounts, the energy, the work and feats of this man will, sometime in the future, be the finish of this now wonderful and famous performer.

The restless striving to do something better than another human being has brought him to the highest pinnacle of fame, has earned for him princely salaries, and when one considers the risks he has taken, no one can begrudge him the prime minister's salary, which he is earning.

To show the restless craving of this man for excelling in things where it is impossible to be of any value to him in any way or form, an incident regarding this man is well worth relating. He was returning from Australia, and the steamer, after leaving Brisbane touched Suva, on the Fiji Islands, a place infested with the most voracious man-eating sharks, known in the world's history. It is stated that they will not touch a black man, and perhaps, that is why the Fiji Islanders stand in no fear of being devoured by sharks, and whenever a shark enters the harbour, it is one of the sights of the country, same as it is in Colombo or Port Said. The Natives dive for coins that the passengers throw overboard. One big fellow seemed to be a most wonderful diver and would always come up with the coin in his mouth, pretending to the average spectator that he had cought the coin in his mouth.

Houdini, being an observant spectator, claimed that the man caught the coins in his hand, that is, picked the coin in the water with his hand and placed it in his mouth. This was disputed. Houdini, being offered to wager that if the man's hands were tied behind his back, which would not impede him in making his dive, that he could not catch the coin in his mouth, and Houdini agreed that he would allow himself to be handcuffed, with his hands behind his back, and that he would come up with the coin in his mouth.

An interpreter was called and the Black agreed to undergo the test. The dive was to be made off the steamer, and the Captain warned Houdini that he stood in grave danger of the sharks.

Undaunted, Houdini went below, donned a bathing suit, had a pair of regulation handcuffs locked behind his back; the Black had his hands tied behind him with a cord—he refused to have the handcuffs placed on him, and he said they were too heavy—two coins were thrown overboard, two splashes were simultaneously heard.

Quick as a tiger's spring the Fiji Islander, with his sleek, glossy body, hurled himself through the air and was beneath the surface of the water even while Houdini was perched for his spring. But the jumps were so quickly made, one after the other, that unless you saw the men as they entered the water, you would have thought that it was one prolonged splash. Thirty seconds passed; neither one of the two men appeared. One minute passed, and the black head of the Fiji Islander came up, almost livid for want of air. Fifteen seconds passed by, and, feet first, up came Houdini.

The Fiji Islander did not have his coin, and it seems that Houdini had gathered both of them and had them in his mouth.

He was drawn up with exciting hurry, for the fins of the sharks were seen moving about with rapidity, and, being hauled on deck, Houdini was declared to have won the wager.

The Black's hands were released, were cut apart, the handcuffs were unlocked from Houdini's wrists, and instead of keeping the money, Houdini made it a present to the Black.

In a private interview, on being asked how he defeated the Black, Houdini said with a good-natured smile, "You can pick up a coin in a glass tank with your hands tied behind your back, because you can use your mouth, teeth and tongue to manipulate the coin, but when you are in an ocean and the coin is falling downwards it is almost next to impossible to catch a coin and bring it up in your mouth."

"You ask me how I did it? I will let you in the secret—I didn't do it at all. When I was under the water I released one of my hands which gave me the use of both of them; I caught my coin and I noticed that the Black was unable to get his coin. I swam after him until he had given up trying to get it, and we had gone down to such a distance that my ears rang, my head was splitting, and all I could see was the white shining piece of money—it was an English two-shilling piece. Eventually I grabbed the coin, put it in my mouth and came up. As I came up, I happened to have my hands free and as I could not stop myself with the force I had sent myself up with my hands I turned around and came up feet first, and this allowed me to put my hands behind my back and the regulation handcuff, as you know, being a snap lock, I locked my hands together and to all intents and purposes my hands were locked during the entire feat. That is why I gave the Fiji Islander the entire amount at stake."

"Was I afraid of the sharks?"

"Yes and No! Being able to see under water, I kept a sharp look-out, and as soon as I would have seen anything that looked like a shark I would have done a record swim to the boat."

"No, I would not care to do it again; it was not for the money, it was simply to show that I was as good a swimmer as some of those Fiji Islanders."

HISTORICAL LOCK PICKERS.

It used to be the fashion among inventors to challenge the trade and other persons, to pick them.

In some cases, even rewards were offered to any one who could do so.

It is believed that Mr. Joseph Bramah was the first to do this and in 1801, he displayed in his shop window in Piccadily, London, a board to which was attached a padlock, manufactured by himself, and which bore the following inscription:—

"The artist who can make an instrument that will pick or open this lock shall receive 200 guineas the moment it is produced."

In 1832, a Wolverhampton locksmith, having claimed to having picked 18 Chubb locks, Mr. Chubb challenged him to open one of his locks under certain conditions.

Mr. Hart tried and failed, giving the explanation that it was not the regular commercial Chubb lock, but one that had a special bridge ward.

Mr. Chubb replied that Mr. Hart did not pick any lock, but made false keys by a process of cutting blanks.

In America the great lock of Dr. Andrews, in 1841, being heralded as an unpickable lock, with two sets of tumblers, was produced, the inventor offering 500 dollars to any one who could pick this.

It was picked by Pettitt and Hall, of Boston, with what is known as the smoke process.

1851. HOBBS PICKS BRAMAH AND CHUBB LOCK.

In 1851 Mr. A. C. Hobbs arrived from America, picked a Chubb lock before a committee, and picked the Bramah lock, winning thereby the 200 guineas that for 50 years no one was able to claim.

Mr. Hobbs offered 200 guineas to anyone who would pick his lock. An engineer named Garbutt, known as an expert, took up the challenge, and failed after trying thirty days.

1855.—YALE PICKS HOBBS' LOCK.

As an additional element to this controversy, in 1855, Linnius Yale, Jr., discovered how to pick the then celebrated Day and Newell Parautoptic Bank Lock.

It was of American origin, and was known in England as Hobbs Lock, but was the invention of a Mr. Pyle.

Yale also discovered that he could pick the best Bank Lock—the Double Treasury, which he himself had designed.

And eventually demonstrated that any lock having a key hole could be opened by any expert with the necessary skill and time at his disposal.

Accordingly Mr. Yale proceeded to develop the combination or Dial Lock.

1870.—SARGENT PICKS YALE LOCK.

The general use of this lock led to the controversy in the United States in 1870; and the Yale lock was picked by James Sargent, of the firm of Sargent and Greenleaf, a lock inventor, a leading maker of Bank Locks, and the inventor of the Time Lock.

1905.—HOUDINI PICKS SARGENT LOCK.

Houdini bearded the lion in his den by escaping from a Police Cell in Rochester, N. Y., which was securely locked with one of the Sargent and Greenleaf Locks, placing himself on record as one of the great lock pickers of the world.

Of the thousands of locks he has picked all over the world, the following police certificates places him among the historical lock pickers, in fact, second to none.

POLICE HEADQUARTERS, ROCHESTER, N. Y. U. S. OF AMERICA.

We, the undersigned, certify that we saw Harry Houdini, the bearer of this note, stripped naked, searched, locked in one of the cells at Police Headquarters, and handcuffed with three pairs of cuffs, also strapped with a strap extending from pair of cuffs and buckled at the back.

He removed the cuffs, unlocked the cell, got into an adjoining cell and returned with his clothes on.

After unlocking the cell in which he was first placed, he had to unlock the cell in which his clothing was left.

This was witnessed by the following persons, at Police Headquarters, this city, December 4th, 1905.

J. C. HAYDEN, Chief of Police.

Mr. James Sargent personally complimented Houdini on his rare skill. They became friends and spent hours together exchanging lock opening secrets.

NOTE.—We beg to acknowledge our indebtedness to the following publications for data used in this article—Price's Book on "Locks and Keys" 1856; New International Encyclopedia 2nd Edition; (Dodd Mead and Co., New York); and Encyclopedia Americana, J. M. Stoddart, 1886.

POLICE HEADQUARTERS, CHICAGO, ILL., U. S. OF AMERICA.

This is to certify that the undersigned saw Harry Houdini stripped stark naked, searched from head to foot, and shackled with handcuffs around the wrists and leg irons around his ankles.

He was then placed in a cell which required TWO LARGE keys of different makes and patterns to open the lock. The keys are of such a nature that it would have been positively impossible for him to have concealed them on his body.

We searched the cell and thoroughly searched Houdini from head to foot, also between his toes and the soles of his feet. Nevertheless in fifteen minutes he managed to release himself from the manacles and make his escape from the cell.

There was positively no chance for outside assistance.

(Signed), ANDREW ROHAN,

Chief of Detectives. Nov. 24, 1906.

The Only Paper in the City that Dares Print the News

LOS ANGELES RECORD

21st Year. WED. DEC. 1, 1915. No. 6485

2,000 HISS J. WILLARD.
CHAMPION DRIVEN FROM THEATER BY HOOTS AND CALLS

Boxing has been given its worst black eye here to-day by none other than Jess Willard, heavy-weight champion who was so badly worsted to a wordy clash with Harry Houdini, a performer at the Orpheum Theater, last night, that the audience hissed him from the house.

Nearly 2,000 persons were present at the dramatic scene and seemed unanimous in groaning, hooting and booing Willard.

The trouble was precipitated by Willard's gruff refusal to comply with a friendly request made by Houdini that he act on a committee to watch the performer's act from the stage.

It was not known that Willard was present until Houdini came before the footlights and requested any "gentleman" in the audience to step on the stage and guard those present from any possible deception.

After about 10 men had stepped on the platform, Houdini stepped forward and said, smiling:

"Now I need three more gentlemen on this stage and there is a man here to-night who doesn't know I am aware of his presence. He will be enough for three ordinary gentlemen if he will serve on this committee."

"He is Jess Willard, our champion."

Taken by surprise, the audience was silent for a moment and then broke into tumultous hand-clapping. Cheers and shrieks resounding throughout the house.

Houdini looked up on the balcony, where Willard was seated, and said:

"I will leave it to the audience, Mr. Willard. You see they want to see you."

A fresh outburst occurred, even more violent than before.

"Aw, g'wan with your act," came Willard's rough reply as the audience stilled itself. "I paid for my seat here."

"But, Mr. Willard," expostulated Houdini, "I—

"Give me the same wages you pay those other fellows and I'll come down," rumbled Willard's deep voice.

The audience, scenting something unusual, was very quiet.

"Sir, I will gladly do so," returned Houdini, heatedly. "Come on down—I pay these men nothing."

"Aw' g'wan with the show," roared Willard, growling something that sounded like "four-flusher" and "faker."

Willard's boorish replies evidently displeased those present, for a few scattering hisses came about this time.

Houdini stepped to the footlights and held up his hand for silence.

It was readily granted.

"Jess Willard, I have just paid you a compliment," said Houdini dramatically. "Now I want to tell you something else.

"I will be Harry Houdini, Jess Willard, when you are NOT the heavyweight champion of the world."

A roar of applause shook the house. Men and women alike joined in the clapping and cheering.

A deep rumble from the balcony indicated that Willard was trying to make some retort, and the cheers veered suddenly to hoots and groans.

"I made a mistake," said Houdini, addressing the audience. "I asked GEN-TLEMEN to step on this stage and GENTLEMEN only."

A renewed outburst occurred, during which Willard evidently left the theater. He was not to be found after the next act had started.

HALF-AN-HOUR WITH HOUDINI, THE EX-PERT OF EXTRICATION

"Danger does not mean anything to me; I was just born without the ingredient of fear. Apart from the many risks I have taken in the course of my professional career, I have saved lives any number of times, and I have simply taken it all as a matter of course. People talk of being afraid to die; on the contrary, I am so well prepared for such an emergency that not only is my will drawn up, but I have a bronze memorial bust all ready, because I thought it better to have one that was really like me!"

THE HANDCUFF KING

Thus spoke Houdini, the "handcuff king," the great magician and genius of escape, on a certain sunny morning a few weeks ago. He sat with his back to the light, but though his face was in shadow the compelling blue grey eyes, and strong, bronzed features glowed with an intensity and vitality such as one rarely meets.

"Tell me," I begged, "are the feats you do on the screen different to those you do enact before the footlights?"

"Entirely different," was the reply.

"In fact, some of the biggest critics have said that I am more wonderful on the screen than on the stage. That, I consider, is one of the greatest compliments ever paid me. But it has taken years of training to produce the tricks, or problems, I do in my films."

Houdini has made, to date, three pictures. The first of these, "The Master Mystery," a serial, is now enjoying enormous popularity all over the country. The remaining two, "The Grim Game," and "Terror Island," are feature pictures, and are still unreleased by Paramount Artcraft though this year will see the first-named on our screens. In the making of "The Master Mystery," Houdini sustained seven black eyes and a broken wrist. He also broke his wrist whilst making "The Grim

Game."

A TENSE MOMENT

"During the screening of this picture I thought at one time in the course of the action, that my end had come," he told me. "I was 3,000 feet up in an aeroplane, circling over another machine. The plan was for me to drop from my 'plane into the cockpit of the other by means of a rope. I was dangling from the rope-end ready for the leap. Suddenly a strong wind turned the lower plane upwards, the two machines crashed together—nearly amputating my limbs—the propellers locked in a deadly embrace, and we were spun round and round and round." Houdini pronounced the latter words with a peculiarly apt "whirring" intonation, graphically illustrating them by the circular action of the arms. "But," he continued, "by a miracle, the 'planes were righted into a half-glide, and, though they were smashed into splinters by their terrific impact, I managed to escape unhurt. As usual, Houdini became undone!" concluded the narrator with a laugh.

HIS GREATEST STUNT

"What do you consider the greatest stunt you have done for the screen?" I asked, when I had recovered my breath.

"Another incident in the same picture," answered Houdini. "I stood in the archway of a prison, thus——" Here he took up a crouching position in the corner of the room, and enacted the whole thing for my benefit. "A heavily loaded lorry, going at twenty-two or four miles an hour rolled by me. I threw myself on the ground, completely rolling over between the fast revolving fore and hind wheels, over and over, till I caught the transmission bar, and hung there for very dear life! Thus was I carried to the aid of the heroine. Though my words may not convey very much, this was my greatest stunt. It allowed for no rehearsals—I said to the camera-man, 'Get this now or never!' And had I made the slightest false move I should have been crippled for life, if not killed."

In spite of the risks he has taken before the camera, Houdini has a profound love and admiration for the "movies."

"I think the film profession is the greatest," he told me "and that the moving picture is the most wonderful thing in the world. One reason why I love the screen is because it has use for the derelicts of life, and gives employment to the old as well as the young. I entered the profession myself because I knew I should eventually be losing my strength, and before that happened I wanted to perpetuate my feats, and by so doing everyone, in all parts of the world, can see them. Pictures have increased my drawing power two-hundredfold."

Houdini, as related at the commencement of this chat, had one of his greatest compliments paid him by critics of his film work, but before I left him he confessed that what he considers the very greatest tribute ever made to his unique achievements is recorded in a dictionary! Turn to Funk and Wagnall's Standard Dictionary, and there you will find it:

"HOU'DI-NI. 1, hu'di-ni;

2, hu'di-ni, HARRY (4-6, 1874). American mystericist, wizard, and expert in extrication and self-release HOU'DI-NIZĒ vt. To release or extricate oneself from (confinement, bonds, or the like), as by wriggling out."

So, taking Houdini all in all, I may consider the fact that this wonder-man, this "expert in extrication," made no effort to escape from at least one thing this interview!

MAY HERSCHEL CLARKE.

Sat.] ROCHESTER EVENING TIMES [Nov. 4
1916

MINISTER USES HOUDINI'S NAME FOR SERMON

His Art of Getting Out of Things as Topic of Sermon

The name of Houdini, who has been a headliner at a local theater this week will figure in the sermon at the Genesee Street Baptist Church, to-morrow morning, where the pastor, Rev. Clark, will talk on "Houdini and the Art of Getting Out of Things." The pastor, however, insures that he will reveal none of the vital points of the art, but declares that the sermon will be entirely spiritual.

THE SUN

Pittsburg Monday, Nov. 6th, 1916

20,000 PEOPLE SEE HOUDINI THRILLING AIR STRUGGLE.

WIZARD TIED IN JACKET IS FREE IN 3 MINUTES.

STRAPPED TIGHTLY BY GUARDS FROM MAYVIEW HE HANGS HEAD DOWN WARD.

SUN BUILDING IS SCENE. WHILE SPINNING DIZZILY FIFTY FEET ABOVE PAVEMENT HE ESCAPES FROM BONDS.

Swaying, head downwards, like a grotesque human pendulum, 50 feet above the pavement in front of The Sun Building, Harry Houdini, "handcuff king," defier of locks, bars and bonds, freed himself from the grip of a canvas, leather-reinforced straight-jacket, in a fraction more than three minutes, shortly after 12.40 o'clock this afternoon.

The waving of his free hands and arms, that a crowd estimated at 20,000 has seen bound by two attendants from the Mayview (old Marshalsea) Hospital for the Insane, told the watchers that Houdini had achieved one of the most unique feats in his strange career. As he was lowered swiftly to the ground, a great cheer arose, followed by another and another as he stood upright and bowed to the throng which not only packed the streets but filled every window and roof top within view of the scene.

WIZARD IS ON TIME

Urbane, smiling, the elusive Houdini appeared in the office of "The Sun" at 12 o'clock. R. D. Polling and H. Guthrie, the two attendants from Mayview detailed to truss him up, awaited him, and with them the straight-jacket, in a satchel.

Houdini shook hands with both men, speaking humorously of his position as substitute for the deranged persons the two Attendants ordinarily handle. The two men, clad in the white uniforms used by them when on duty, surveyed their voluntary victim noted his short, stocky form, his powerful arms and shoulders, his steady, bright eyes.

Both have had long experience in binding frenzied men. Both were determined, they told Houdini, to use the full resource of that experience in binding him. They knew the prowess of the man they had to deal with. They did not comment upon the outcome of the test.

They were there, they said, to do their work as best they knew how.

Houdini urged speed of action, and absolute surety in fastening the innumerable straps of the straight-jacket.

"Treat me," he advised, smiling, "as you would the most dangerous of the criminal insane."

EVERY MOVE IS WATCHED

The strait-jacket was taken out of the satchel. The handcuff king examined it carefully, while a group of persons looked on. Not a move he made was lost. He dropped the piece of canvas and leather carelessly, smiled again, and said:

"Very good. Are we ready?"

It was almost 12.30 o'clock. Houdini glanced out the window, and again his characteristic, quiet smile came to his face as he saw Wood street and Liberty avenue congested from wall to wall with closely packed, restless humanity.

Then a white-clad attendant on each side, he went downstairs to the street to be bound.

A suppressed shout came from the crowd as he appeared in the doorway of The Sun building. It increased in volume as with the attendants and two members of "The Sun" at 12 o'clock. R. D. Polling wagon that had been pulled up on the pavement, and that was serving as a stage.

Above him, like a gallows, a single beam projected from a window at the top story of the building, and a rope swung clear, coiling in sinister fashion at his feet.

Houdini had removed the outer clothing from the upper part of his body.

"Ready," he said.

STRAPS ARE FASTENED

The two attendants pressed close. His arms were inserted in the long, closed sleeves of the straitjacket. One of the attendants clasped him about the body, as if fearing he would make some mad effort to escape. The other standing behind him, fastened strap after strap, with a steady deftness that made both for security and speed, and revealed long practice.

"Make it tight," came the quiet word from the prisoner.

The man's knees went up for purchase in the small of Houdini's back. Using apparently every ounce of strength in his broad-shouldered six-foot body, the attendant drew the big strap through the buckle until it would not yield even a sixteenth of an inch more. He caught it there and made it fast.

Then the arms of the prisoner were crossed over his body, and the ends of those closed sleeves were brought around in back. Again the knee was brought into use. Again the strap was pulled to its highest tension.

The crowd watched, stirred with a constant murmur and movement.

Then Houdini's ankles were fastened to the rope, by a special appliance that prevented injury, but insured safety.

A word was spoken. The two attendants seized the bound man's body. Workmen drew the rope steadily through the pulleys. Houdini's feet went up, and as his body cleared the platform, it was released.

HANGS IN MID-AIR

The handcuff king dangled head downward. Each moment he was drawn higher, swaying slightly, spinning dizzily. Up-up, past the windows in the fifth story of the Sun building. Houdini was drawn.

Then he hung still.

Only for a second. While watchers gleamed in the crowd below, the handcuff king was seen to struggle, not frantically, but with a steady, systematic swelling and contracting of muscles, and almost imperceptible lithe, wrigglings of the tor-so.

The struggle went on. One minute — two — then three — —

Would he do it? Hundreds in the crowd undoubtedly were asking that question. From above came an inarticulate shout. The muffled arms writhed one after another over Houdini's head. His hand, still encased in the sleeves of the strait-jacket, fumbled quickly and effectively with the buckles at his back. Another contortion and the strait-jacket slipped down over his chest, over his head, and was flung from his arms to the street, in a crumpled heap.

Houdini was free.

The arms waved. Houdini had triumphed — as he always triumphs.

Less than a minute later, while the crowd's cheers still rang against the grey walls of surrounding buildings, he slipped down the face of the building to the platform. The attendants received him in a twinkling, and he stood erect, unconsciously throwing back his broad shoulders.

The little man with the touch of grey at his temples bowed quietly, still with that imperturbable smile. And the crowd cheered him again, before it began slowly to dissolve.

Houdini duplicated this feat at the Boston Post, Boston, Mass., December 22, 1921, drawing the biggest crowd that ever crushed into Tremont Street.

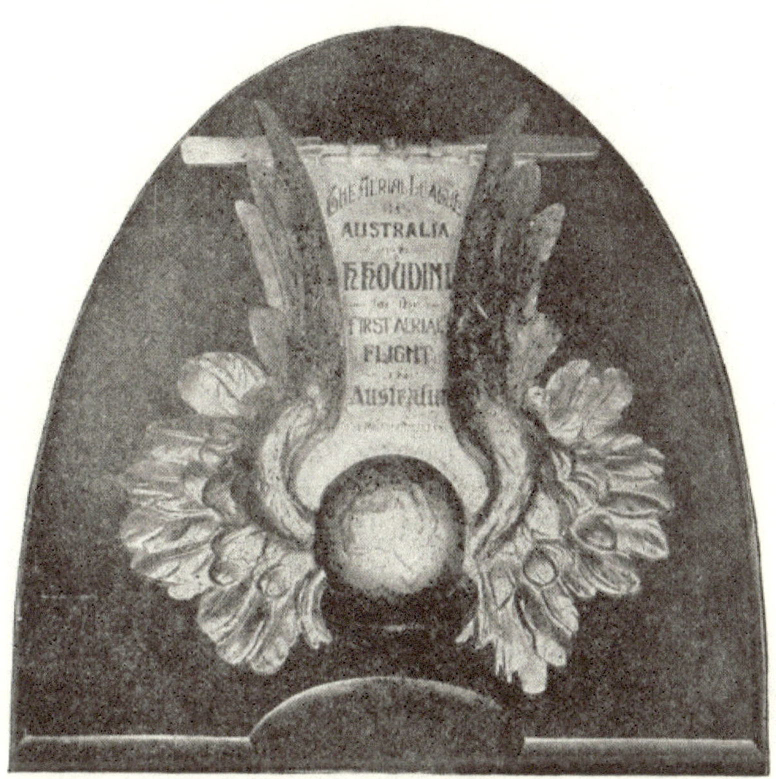

Trophy won by Houdini.

The accompanying illustration is the prize offered by the Australian Aerial League for the first successful flight on a heavier than air machine. Won by Houdini March 16, 1910, Digger's Rest, near Melbourne Australia. Houdini piloted his own machine—a Voision Biplane equipped with a E.N.V. 60.80 H.P. Motor. During his Australian Tour Houdini made 18 successful flights.

LONDON, ENGLAND

HOLBORN EMPIRE BESIEGED BY CROWD INSIDE AND OUTSIDE—UNPAR-
ALLELED SCENES WITNESSED IN HIGH HOLBORN—POLICE RESERVES
CALLED OUT

A packed house, to show its disapproval of the management's action, remains at the Holborn Empire, from 2:00 to 9:00 P. M., waiting for Houdini's appearance as advertised. Police forces were called out as the matinee crowd, refusing to leave the theatre, the evening crowd blockaded traffic, being unable to gain admittance. Unparalleled scenes witnessed in High Holborn.

"THE PERFORMER" LONDON ENGLAND,
DECEMBER 15, 1910.

A STAND FOR JUSTICE - HOUDINI'S PRO-TEST

"For some mysterious reason, surprisingly little attention has been given in the daily papers to a remarkable 'scene' at the Holborn Empire last Thursday, when Houdini made a plucky and public-spirited protest against prevailing matinee methods. We must, we suppose, attribute to the present obsession of politics the scant attention given to a very unusual incident, of interest alike to the public and the profession.

"Having received an intimation from the management that, although he was topping the week's bill, his services would not be required at the Thursday matinee, 'owing to the length of the programme,' Houdini expressed himself perfectly agreeable to this arrangement, subject to the condition that due intimation should be given to the public that he would not be appearing.

"This condition not being complied with, he took an opportunity of going on to the stage at the conclusion of one of the matinee turns in order to quietly explain the reason for his non-appearance and to show that it was not his fault that he was breaking faith with the public. He did not urge the audience, as was stated in some reports, to stay until he appeared, but said that he assumed some at least had come to see him perform and that it seemed to him such were certainly to have their money back if they did not see him.

"The performance went on quietly until 'God Save the King,' when the audience took the matter into its own hands and refused to disperse, calling for Houdini to appear. After a scene of considerable excitement, 150 persons ultimately accepted the management's offer of vouchers for another performance and left the building, but the great bulk of the audience remained until after the conclusion of Houdini's performance at the first evening house, when they trooped out, leaving the place only a quarter full.

"The queues which formed up for the first house had in the main to be accommodated at the second house, and great difficulty was experienced in controlling the further arrivals for the second performance.

"The audience's just appreciation of Houdini's protest was voiced in the remarks of a Labor leader who helped to beguile the interval between the afternoon and evening houses by making a speech. He said that he had frequently attended such matinees, and had always attributed the frequent failure of some one or more well-known artists to appear to his (or her) personal indifference or indolence, but that now they knew the real reason why the public were disappointed.

"In view of a managerial allegation to the afternoon audience that Houdini was not allowed to appear because he had broken his contract, we quote from a further considered protest with which Houdini prefaced his performance at the first house in the evening. He said:

"'Before proceeding with my performance this evening, I believe that there is an explanation due to a great many who are assembled here as to the cause of my non-appearance here this afternoon, and if it would interest you to hear, I will explain. I wish to inform you that it is positively no fault of mine, because I was here in the building, ready to work, but the management refused to allow me to go on. I will read a number of letters that I have here, which thoroughly explain the case, and I wish to inform you that I have played a good many weeks on this tour, and never knew exactly where I was going until a few days ahead. I was billed to appear at the Holborn a short time ago, and, without any notification whatever, I was sent to Woolwich, and the public received no explanation why I did not appear here.

"'Very likely a great many thought that I had broken faith with the public, and last night I received a letter—dated the 6th—after the second performance (about 11 o'clock) which was 33 hours later than dated, notifying me that my services were not required for the matinee performance.'

"Having quoted this letter and his reply stating the condition on which he was agreeable to the arrangement, Houdini continued:

"'Now, ladies and gentlemen, I wanted to keep faith with the public, and informed the management that I would give the salary that I was earning at the matinee to the V. A. B. F. if they would only allow me to appear, as I knew my reputation was at stake. Being billed, and not appearing, what would the public think? Despite this, I was not allowed to appear, and I trust that those who are assembled here this evening will see my motive in allowing the public to know the real cause of my non-appearance, and that it was positively not my fault.'

"The first result of this dignified protest was that Houdini's services were, notwithstanding notice to the contrary, requisitioned for the Saturday matinee."

Houdini, in his speech to the audience that evening, was forcible and to the point, informing them that it was the greatest compliment that had ever been paid him—an audience waiting seven hours in a theatre for him—and that he would never forget it—and he never will.

Boston Daily Globe, March 19, 1906.

HOUDINI ESCAPES FROM CITY PRISON

Handcuffed, Ironed, and Locked in Cell, He takes only 16 Minutes to Get Out and over the Wall

Harry Houdini, the young man who, apparently, cannot be held in restraint by steel bars, handcuffs, prison locks, or other restraining measures, gave the Boston Police Department a terrific jolt this forenoon when he escaped from double confinement in the city prison, commonly known as the Tombs, a prison which the heads of the police department had confidently believed to be escape proof.

SUPT. WILLIAM H. PIERCE, WHO LOCKED CELL DOORS

Superintendent of Police William H. Pierce personally superintended the confinement of Houdini, himself locked the wizard into a cell on the second tier of the prison, after he had clamped handcuffs on his wrists and leg irons about his ankles, and the superintendent's face wore a smile of confidence and assurance after he had locked the cell doors and went down into the office of the prison to await results.

The superintendent's smile didn't wholly come off when, a few minutes later, he learned that Houdini not only had escaped from his cell, but that he had escaped from the prison, and was nearly a half-mile away; but the smile was faded and frayed at the edges, and no questioning could get the superintendent to say what he thought of the wonderful performance. All that could be gotten out of him was, "I have nothing to say."

Heretofore the police have believed that no one locked in a cell at the Tombs could possibly get out; but Houdini not only got out, but he opened door after door after he had removed the handcuffs and leg irons, and walked from one part of the prison to another with apparently as much freedom as though he wasn't met every few feet with a lock that had been considered impregnable.

CLOSELY SEARCHED FOR KEYS.

Briefly, here is just what happened: Houdini had secured permission from Superintendent Pierce to make an effort to escape from the city prison, and this forenoon, in the presence of about 30 men, the superintendent let Houdini into cell No. 77 on the ground floor of the Tombs, where Houdini, in the presence of the witnesses of the test, removed every stitch of his clothing, which he left lying on the bunk in the cell. When he came out, Capt. Clarence A. Swan, the keeper of the prison, locked the cell door upon Houdini's clothing, and then the young man was taken to the second floor of the block of cells, where Superintendent Pierce and a number of the men witnessing the test searched his hair for possible concealed keys or other instruments. Not a thing was found, and Houdini even asked to have his feet examined so there would be no question of his having a key concealed between his toes, and this was done.

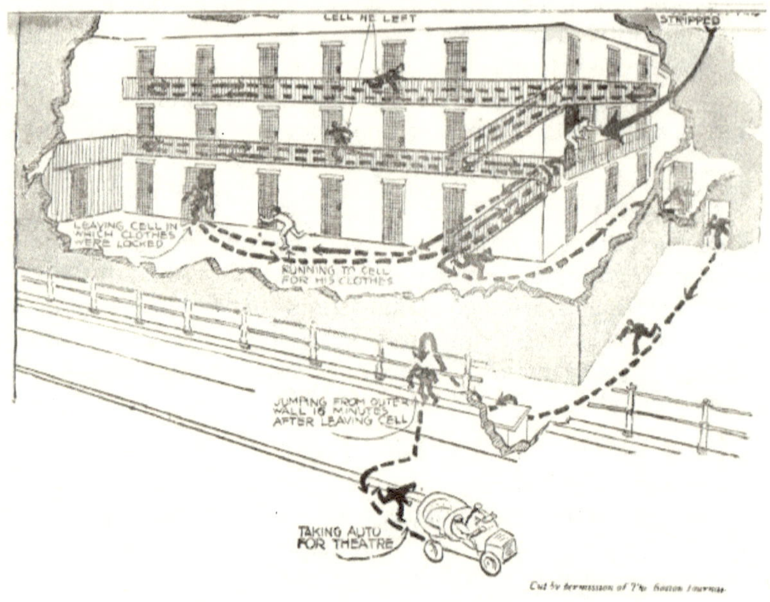

Boston Journal, Tuesday, March 20, 1906.

SHACKLED AND LOCKED IN, HOUDINI BREAKS JAIL. CENTRAL FIGURES IN WIZARD HOUDINI'S MYSTIFYING JAIL ESCAPE AND DIAGRAM OF HIS MOVEMENTS.

Cut by permission of The Boston Journal.

Inside the Cell at the City Tombs, Boston, Mass.

SUP'T. PIERCE LEFT HIM SHACKLED AND HANDCUFFED IN CELL No. 60

SUP'T. PIERCE SAT CHUCKLING IN THE CAPTAIN'S OFFICE WAITING FOR HOUDINI TO WHISTLE FOR HIM.

**IN SIXTEEN MINUTES AFTER BEING LOCKED UP HE ES-
CAPED OVER THE WALL.**

THE SUP'T. FOUND THE SHACKLES AND HANDCUFFS—BUT NO HOUDINI.

Caricatures by permission of Boston Post.

Then Superintendent Pierce took a pair of the most approved handcuffs used in the police department and fastened them securely about Houdini's wrists, and on his bare ankles he clamped a pair of tested steel leg irons so tightly that the iron sank into the flesh. After that Houdini was locked in cell No. 60, and Superintendent Pierce and the witnesses went downstairs and out into the office, expecting

Houdini would go there, providing he got out of his cell, and the police officials who were present seemed to feel pretty confident that he couldn't do that. This feeling was shared by some of the outsiders present, who could not bring themselves to believe that it could be done.

Over the Wall at the City Tombs, Boston, Mass.
Photo with permission of the Boston Globe.

The only condition Houdini attached to his performance was that no one should be allowed to go into the part of the prison where he was confined to watch him escape, and the superintendent and the witnesses respected that condition, and most of them stayed in the captain's office. A few of the witnesses, however, went out into Somerset Street to wait and watch; for, knowing Houdini, they were prepared to see him come out anywhere.

These confident ones were rewarded for their trust, for 16 minutes after Houdini had been locked, naked, handcuffed, and ironed by the legs, into cell 60, he was seen running, fully dressed, except that he had not put on his collar and tie, across the prison yard, to climb up the wall leading into Somerset Street, to vault the iron railing at the top, and then to leg it like a scared rabbit over the hill in the direction of Keith's Theatre.

THE LITERARY HOUDINI

As is the case with many great men, the gift of being able to do many things, and to do each thing well, is Houdini's, who besides his achievements as a mystifier has also won wide recognition as an author. That he has found time to write a great deal is attested by his list of books, namely: "Miracle Mongers and Their Methods," "The Unmasking of Robert Houdin," "The Sane Side of Spiritualism," "The Right Way to do Wrong," "Magic Made Easy," "My Training and my Tricks," "Paper Prestidigitation," "Handcuff Secrets," "Magical Rope Ties and Escapes," "Good Night Stories for Children," "Dan Cupid the Magician" (a series) and "Magicians' Romances." Numerous magazine articles and stories swell his literary output to greater proportions. Editor for two years on standard work of magic, "The Conjurors Magazine."

In addition he has also written the stories for the feature films in which he was starred, namely, "The Man From Beyond" and "Haldane of the Secret Service," which were picturized by his own producing organization, Houdini Picture Corporation; "The Grim Game" and "Terror Island," written in collaboration with Arthur B. Reeve and John W. Grey, produced by Famous Players-Lasky Corporation.

HOUDINI PICTURE CORPORATION

In 1921, upon returning from his triumphant tour of Great Britain, Houdini organized his own film producing company for the purpose of making special feature pictures. The company, incorporated as Houdini Picture Corporation, capitalized at $500,000, began operations in the spring.

At the time of this writing two features have been completed—"The Man from Beyond" and "Haldane of the Secret Service." The first is characterized by those who have seen it at private pre-release showings as the most unusual picture ever screened, containing, as it does, originality of thought, novelty of treatment, and a thrilling finish that encompasses any thrilling situation yet produced for motion pictures.

The second picture, with interlocking scenes taken abroad, tells a mystery story and likewise demonstrates the ingenuity and resourcefulness of Houdini as producer, author and star.

Both pictures will soon be released to the public.

SCENES FROM PHOTOPLAYS

JESSE L. LASKY
Presents

HOUDINI

IN

"THE GRIM GAME"

A Paramount-Artcraft Picture

This picture contains the only airplane collision in the clouds ever photographed.

$1,000 reward to anyone proving the collision in the clouds is not genuine.

STARRING HOUDINI

JESSE L. LASKY
Presents

HOUDINI

IN

"TERROR ISLAND"

A Paramount-Artcraft
Picture

The most amazing under water scenes ever enacted were recorded by the camera for "Terror Island."

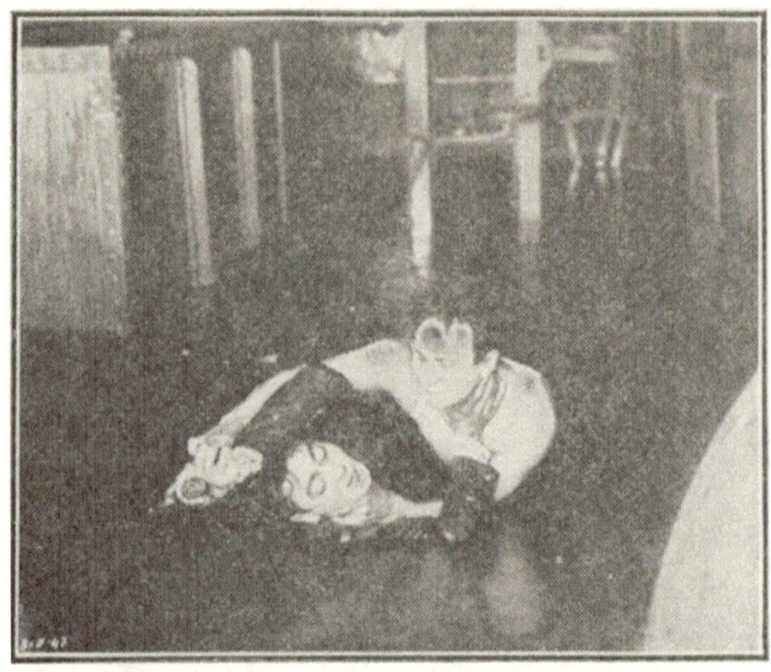

SCENES FROM PHOTOPLAYS

HOUDINI PICTURE
CORP.

Presents

HOUDINI

in

"THE MAN FROM BEYOND"

*Shortly to be
Released*

Starring Houdini

HOUDINI PICTURE

CORP.
Presents

HOUDINI

in

"HALDANE OF THE SECRET SERVICE"

*An International
Mystery Drama
shortly to be released.*

PICTURE PLAYS, CONFESSIONS ALBUM.
NO. 14.—MR. HARRY HOUDINI

1. What is your favorite theater?

All the world is a theater to me.

2. Which is your favorite hobby?

Browsing in old bookstalls, seeking old dramatic items for my library.

3. Which is your favorite pastime?

Out door athletics and long distance swims.

4. Which is your favorite song?

"Auld Lang Syne."

5. Which is your favorite sweetmeat?

Candied fruits.

Mrs. HARRY HOUDINI

6. What is your idea of comfort?

Seated in a large arm chair in library and hearing Mrs. Houdini call up: "Young man your lunch is ready."

7. Which is your unlucky day?

Haven't any; an unfortunate incident at any time simply builds a foundation for something better.

8. What is your favorite motto?

"And this, too—shall pass away."

9. When have you felt at your worst?

Once when sailing round the world, at a longitude of 80°, we had two Tuesdays in one week and no Wednesday, which meant losing a Christmas, and I was seasick at the time. It will be an awful thing to eclipse my painful anguish.

10. What is your pet aversion?

The bald-headed man who says: "Ah, I remember you when I was a boy."

MY MOTHER

11. What is your greatest ambition?

To live a life and die being worthy of the mother who bore me.

12. What is your favorite holiday resort?

Hollywood, California.

13. Who is your favorite author?

My dad.

14. What is your idea of misery?

Arriving in a town at midnight on a drizzly wet, foggy night, and finding all the hotels full up.

Snap shot photograph of packing case containing six hundred pounds of iron weights and Houdini, as it was dropped into New York Bay. Houdini escaped from the box at the bottom of the bay in two minutes

and fifty-five seconds.

DR. WILLIAMS ENGINEERING THE "THREAD THE NEEDLES TRICK"

HOUDINI ABOUT TO DISAPPEAR

WELL, GOODBYE

The National Casket Company challenged Houdini to escape from one of their heavy hickory coffins after they had fastened the cover down with six inch screws. Houdini accepted the test, which took place before members of the Boston Athletic Association, Boston, Mass. He escaped, the coffin was intact, showing no means of egress.

MR. PHIL SEARS

MR. COTTON

INTERESTED SPECTATORS IN THE FRONT ROW.

A LITTLE MORE AIR FOR MR. HOUDINI

THE HAGGARD HOUDINI REAPPEARS

HOPE I GET OUT OF MINE AS QUICKLY

HOW DOES HE DO IT?

JAMES H. HARRIS,
WARDEN,

W. GRAYSON URNER,

DEPUTY WARDEN,

UNITED STATES JAIL,

Washington, D.C., January 6th, *1906*

This is to certify that Mr. Harry Houdini, at the United States Jail today, was stripped stark naked, thoroughly searched, and locked up in cell No. 2 of the South Wing, — the cell in which Charles J. Guiteau, the assassinator of President Garfield, was confined during his incarceration, from the date of his commitment, July 2nd, 1881, until the day on which he was executed, June 30th, 1882. Mr. Houdini, in about two minutes, managed to escape from that cell, and then broke into the cell in which his clothing was locked up. He then proceeded to release from their cells all the prisoners on the ground floor. There was positively no chance for any confederacy or collusion.

Mr. Houdini accomplished all of the above-mentioned facts, in addition to putting on all his clothing, in twenty-one minutes.

J. H. Harris

Warden United States Jail, D. C.

Lector House believes that a society develops through a two-fold approach of continuous learning and adaptation, which is derived from the study of classic literary works spread across the historic timeline of literature records. Therefore, we aim at reviving, repairing and redeveloping all those inaccessible or damaged but historically as well as culturally important literature across subjects so that the future generations may have an opportunity to study and learn from past works to embark upon a journey of creating a better future.

This book is a result of an effort made by Lector House towards making a contribution to the preservation and repair of original ancient works which might hold historical significance to the approach of continuous learning across subjects.

HAPPY READING & LEARNING!

LECTOR HOUSE LLP
E-MAIL: lectorpublishing@gmail.com

9 789388 321051